DIVINATIONS

DIVINATIONS

ALLAN BROWN

Ekstasis Editions

Canadian Cataloguing in Publication Data

Brown, Allan
  Divinations

  Poems.
  ISBN 1-896860-29-X

    I. Title.
  PS8553.R6848D58 1998   C811'.54   C98-910197-5
  PR9199.3.B6974D58   1998

© Allan Brown, 1998.
Cover Art: Pat Brown

Acknowledgements:
Most of these poems have appeared in different contexts in my other
books and chapbooks: *Figures of Earth* (Nebula, 1979), *By Green
Mountain* (Penumbra, 1980), *Locatives* (Nebula, 1982), *This Stranger
Wood* (Quarry, 1982), *Winter Journey* (Quarry, 1984), *The Almond Tree*
(Quarry, 1985), *The Burden of Jonah ben Amittai* (Quarry, 1991),
Forgetting (Nebula, 1991), *Ad Libitum* (Hawthorne, 1997), *Shape and
Shade* (Oel, 1998). Some previously uncollected poems have appeared
in *The Antigonish Review, Dandelion, The Malahat Review, The
Nashwaak Review, Nebula* Netzine, *Next Exit, Poetry Canada, The
Prairie Journal of Canadian Literature, Quarry.*

No book is made alone, of course, and I've been particularly lucky in the
company of my editors. So thanks again to Bill Barnes, Barry Dempster,
John Flood, Bob Hilderley, Richard Olafson, Paul Schwartz, and Ken
Strange, and a special word also to Amy Friedman Fraser for her help
with the *Garden or Wilderness?* question.

Published in 1998 by:
Ekstasis Editions Canada Ltd.   Ekstasis Editions
Box 8474, Main Postal Outlet   Box 571
Victoria, B.C. V8W 3S1   Banff, Alberta T0L 0C0

Divinations has been published with the assistance of a grant from the
Canada Council and the Cultural Services Branch of British Columbia.

THE CANADA COUNCIL | LE CONSEIL DES ARTS
FOR THE ARTS | DU CANADA
SINCE 1957 | DEPUIS 1957

for Pat

Hortus conclusus, fons signatus

Contents

Garden or Wilderness?

Both garden and wilderness are a part of each of us. They are what we see and also the way we see. Neither can be located precisely nor can either precisely be known. Their shapes are changeable, their edges uncertain, their innards tangled and dense. Wilderness is the garden's potential; the forms actualize the source. Each interprets the other, but wilderness as the absolute abstraction is also the source of all definitions, both of itself and of its other.

All growth articulates itself by proceeding into, and by means of, some form or limit. This growth is not necessarily a movement upward to something more perfect or even better than it once was. After all, decay is also a part of growth, and decomposition and eventual disappearance are as well. Growth establishes its own pattern, even though we can never know its fulness, for when we see one aspect of growth clearly, another will be hidden or obscured. The border, or shape of the whole, is always just out of sight.

Garden and wilderness have been with us for a long time. The earliest epic hero, Gilgamesh, en route to the Land of Life with his companion Enkidu, confronts and destroys the monster Huwawa (who may also be the monster Gilgamesh) in a cedar forest. The hunter Actaeon rests a moment before his death by the Orchomenian spring. The Old Fellow (Laotzu) rides out smiling on his water buffalo into the wastelands of north-western China. Moses and David, Elijah and Jesus, leave what they know, for a time at least, to meet themselves in the wilderness; and, more recently, Ambrose Bierce enters the drylands of northern Mexico, either to find the others or to be found by them. Owly Lilith, Adam's first wife, was expelled before him from the earliest garden. The author of *Job* and Isaiah the prophet were both familiar with her night magic and desert places, though Isaiah also promised that in its proper time that wilderness would rejoice and bloom *quasi rosum*.

Each day dies with sleep yet the dream renews. The journies outward continue till outward becomes inward as everything comes in its own time to its own kind of home. Garden and wilderness are one.

Naming Autumn

Walking for awhile in the creaky garden this afternoon and I
thought of how old Rikyu first swept the path clean and then
shook down a few leaves to make a more hospitable sight for
his guests.

The water is quiet now,
the trees are dark and
some leaves at the roadside; a couple
of days before/after the full.

Forgotten days   (I mean
the effort of remembering)
how the wind in the stars
(it seems).   Not very many.

The name of autumn
in this shape of trees.
Something written, but
interpretations and forecasts
are deceptive.

      I glance
over my shoulder and along the road:
Basho or nobody there.

Congregation of leaves
at the stream's edge; the empty house.

Images return

The Oracle

from his dark unbeautiful cave
sways tumid and desiring.
Tense fingers raise.
        He moves
resistless to the trodden place,
frowning in this unaccustomed light;

approaching, chooses whether this
or whether this was meant
to sign and fill each shadow.

Item: to live again
if fingers may find
the centre of the red stone.

Morning glistens;
again the keening bird;
back returns the unfamiliar god.

Actaeon

Death is that discovery. When the long
grey light becomes again articulate
in morning half a wind
beyond the edge of day

his dream renews: the pale volcanic stone,
scintillae turning in the hidden air,
her slim legs sweating in
the shadow of the pool.

There was a valley thickly overgrown
with swelling pitchpine and with sharp-needled
cypress trees alien
in the sunlight; a cave

of pale volcanic stone; amphorae dark
with honey; cool emerging water flowed
into the hidden pool
and settled in silence.

He walks uncertainly, gaping, day-blind,
as gently the dry fingers of the leaves
loosen his dusty legs,
and a grass tip enters

like a sparrow the spectre of his dark
decaying mouth. Wait. Somewhere the white moon
is summoning a charm
to each forgetfulness:

redeemable if ever only by
release into the dream where no word is,
returning with the grey-
foot dawn. The edge of day

reduces now to the simplicity
of equal waters waiting in the sun,
Actaeon torn beneath
the intricate red boughs.

Approaching Santa Fé

The sudden dark: and
somewhere a memory
or not quite voice repeating
the dark and the dark's name
through immediate, unperceivable seasons
in this evacuated place, this space
between rain;
       quiet again;
same place, same stupid evening
recovered and slowly forgotten, like
the sharp coyote yap
          till he breaks
soft, slow and in pieces (I can only
see him in pieces, I mean)
like the frizzle-end dancing of a fire
still one and clear in the morning,
defining but not moving toward
my own edge and darkness;
and my foot slips in the sand,
boot sucks; nothing else.

Lilith

Well, flower-face,
there is a small grey thing
squirms in your beak tonight
one further sigh to hell,
whose startled breath becomes
now only a gesture
of the brief darkness.

I wake for a minute,
shivering in the fall
of broken leaves;
tatters of dry moss
make a new and again
a new pattern; the heavy air;
and a few bent stars remember
the Hunter.

    Quietly
in the eternal question
how is known ever
a place, a word or two;
or, for that matter,
whatever chance may come
huge as an owl to bear it out
until the ending of the night,
sustaining in whatever sight
the secret birth of pain.

Yet there is a kind
of soft forgetting
purely inhabits
this restless flame.
My naked face, chop
fall'n turns again;
and if my eyes return,
I'll be seeing you.

The Clearing
near Banff

Any clearing
is ambiguous,
just
as the trail seen
opening
is not what
trail of that
strange return; in
the deep place
between the scattter
of ordinary leaves,
to capture
the single and
imageless
growing heart.

Pruning

I am urged into tree,
to the cling of it, awkward
as caught sunlight in some
improbable definition
of the thick, late spring;
and stagger through the big
branches, my breath now only
an uncertain counting after April
and the day half gone.

The hoarse sun chants
beyond my matchstick movements as
I slash I bend break throw
to the dim ground these branches
in a dustgreen rage.
                    Meanwhile
my industrious disapproving neighbour
glances over to frown at this ravage;
and after a benevolent minute
his daughter straightens up
with the singing white skin
of her pants loosening
wrinkling into a frown.

And I try it again,
pointing with the cut branches:
"This one?" "This one?"
and "no" "yes" is mouthed
behind the green shadows
of my kitchen window;
until I lean forward reaching
for my cut
      but hands contract
from my lord the peach tree
and tendons shake and
I blink in the sunlight
praying for the night to come.

Divinations

Strands of some long-haired moss
dampening under this split willow
branch;
    the afternoon lowers
to a balance of pale blue sky,
till something full of soft
plumping sounds breaks here
and there into my silence;

the stubbled, almost grey folds
of grass on the other side
of the river, wrinkled into the bank,
it seems, like strained, weary cloth;

the sun isn't as hot now;
a drift of midges blurs
the horizon; the lemon-coloured water
no longer moving; a beetle
staggers across the whitened stones.

Melons

I remember the crispy skin
of vast pale melons,
motionless shaded in
however that summer was,
or might become, if some
provocative word
would change memory
to meaning and the proud thing
quiver into this
and this appearing.

Or we have waited too long
perhaps, for suddenly one
brilliant thirst to engrail
memory and meaning,
and the bold hand is stayed,
is weighed in melon pause,
centre and turning, in-
differently urges to
enter the dark sky
and lean wetness of here
the particular trees.

And our recovery in this
unearned extravagance
shapes now the gotten days
in a scatter of rain,
deciding one for one
each journey delicate
as wax, whose ending is
unknowable;
    till
nothing other seems so deep
and dim, and they become
our consonance, receptive
as mirrors, to centre
and return
the immaculate fire.

Die Gold Orangen
for Hugo Wolf

Do you know that country
where his dream is spoken
in ever golden this
now (though no return from)
in-folding-flower-time,

until the time of my
return: kennst du es wohl?
until the urge turns back
from oblivion in
red flower, red flower

under that quiet tree
Dahin: when the wind cries,
in whatever silence
maintain the innocent
eye (beyond the hope of)

wo die Zitronen blühn
and the even pacing
white clouds indifferent
divide (where is my light?)
divide, where is my light?

Midsummer

The losening stars
divide me, merging
these scattered memories
like interchanging
day and day of mid-
summer unquietly
aware, subside
to the mulch of whose
slim bones crackling in
ever this place where
the sweating Archer
rested; and both
content now to wait
through the heather-red
passing of the stupid
moon
   selah

The sound of bees
centres my wonder;
here is the lost
thing almost plain;
I hear your voice
between the half wind
rising, what pause?

and how the startled
almond flowering,
and how the vacant
green and soft grey
fingers of the leaves
caress my throat,
repeat our small veins
image and gain,
as all left particles
of once our effortless
contention beyond
each new margin tensed,
resilient as sand
to a slow wave's breaking
in endless this scatter, year
and days of:
    who?
I raise my head
to the forgotten call

what ghost is this?

Enna

And freshly still the sight of her
shapes carefully that near
and entering road;
my thick pulse catching
(What do you see?) hints,
scraps of the poppy-wet
incongruous field
of myth-darkened Enna
whose minute aligns
this uncertain body,
urging memory
into immediate form
to reach here if here only
a pause of why
the strange making.

Red clouds fail
before the taken dark;
no known place now,
guess or entrance
into whatever day,
until the long fingers
of this tree pierce
my door like a grave
and I wake I see
the altering moon
suspended over
the extended fibres
of once that clearing,
the intricate
layers of cedar
almost visible
in the little dirt,
almost remembering
some last dry seeds
of summer, luminous
ejaculate

rising through the warm-
made-immaculate sea
to wonder again
the gain or loss of:

further now into
her placeless story
to reach a close
of that curious search
for the day's end
and once limit. It
will not be long
till her dying.

The brightness dims;
the ring shakes softly
into deeper night;
the nimbus clears.

The Flight into Egypt

They travelled into
the odour of the night,
their footsteps echoing
the angel's voice;

their dread behind, that death
still somehow to come;
the clearway persisting
in a faint trickle
of the dim path,
illuminated
by a fragment
of the slim moon only
in deepening cloud;

yet her faith like soft eyes
in fear and wonder
equally contained
as that night ended;

timorous even
at the child's quick laughter,
as a myrrh tree made
a funny face at him
in the early dawn.

Wild Rhubarb

How the thick ribs
leaving, splitting
of this wild rhubarb
heave and darken
as the wind catches,
releasing an arc
of hidden growth,
forward and back as
the agitated bush
dips under sun-
fall, scattering
into shape again,
red as the marrow
of the broken dirt.

Still Life: Siliquae

The rundle of drying pods curls
into life again, expected lines
of definition echoing as
my cat-fall-touch anticipates
blunt sperms spattering through
this thickening light; and how
some day yet, and clots of
damp thistle seed sagging
into the new-broken dirt;
the planes of red and black
articulated bones, the scar,
and a carcass of these flowers
or fragments of decaying wood,
finite brown globules
in the sun; the October
darkness of this afternoon.

Untitled

The nones of this unlikely tree
not yet resolved, shaped
against the thickening sky;
its grey scales in focus,
the heavier branches starting
to droop into the empty
shadows of the dirt, and
a hard white crack at the start
of the graft; with no movement
other than somewhere a faint
crinkle of distant voices
breaking the last surface
of this long afternoon
like bubbles of cooling yeast.

Red Akki

That unexpected fruit
before the dark,
how
 the centre
of the heart is
a strange day
remembered.

The slow walls
of voices in
likeness and
unlikeness shifting
into some other
figure now, gapes
to contain both
the split leaf
and symmetrical
water drop.

 And
whatever silence
in the centre
of the breath
shapes brightly
that word again
to be something
like red akki
suddenly
at the mid place
of dying
 all
flame.

Picking Apples

Another season of them soon
enough scattered beneath the looped,
lackadaisical branches
a dozen or so each day,
bitter and unbitten; the birds
having, as usual, more sense,
watching with an ill-concealed
disdain as one after
a couple again I gather
the wormy, misshapen fruit,
crawling groundily away
from this gawking, un-cut-
downable scraggle; around,
between and nearly patient back
to what the apple tree itself
is doing, having its rhythm
and eating it too; it grows
and, incidental
as poems, they drop.

Consider the Lillies

The gathering's always
the problem, not the guarding,
easy enough as long as

a word of lucent dying
in that second scrawl,
and my lover's odour
round as earths'
imagined coronal;
a crooked scimitar
to slice the silken cushion,
or slump of clay
unspun,
a modest Solomon
whose dibble's yet enough
for pushing up daisies;

and pluck'd, return 'em
white against white and
the night coming, uncountable.

The Old Fellow

Loafing for a minute or two
at the gate, toll paid, getting
his papers in order, Laotzu
spoke to the border guard, somewhat
unwillingly, about the way
of yielding; his 3-day beard
browned like a dried cauliflower,
his eyes smarting a little
in the sunlight, he drinks
the last bottle of Westminster
Sherry and rides into the desert.

The Stone

Then Jesus was led by the Spirit
out into the wilderness

I was hungry, admittedly;
after forty days and nights
(the nights were bad) who
wouldn't be? I took the stone
he gave me
     pausing
how long a time to fill
mind's pale mirror?
enduring whatever
expectancy, insect-cautious
to see the angels
of morning with emerald eyes.

Yet it's a gentle thing
to dull the flashing sky,
cool on my skin
     and I
remember even now
the taking of each sinew
and (almost) the cold
embrace of death upon
the first word of me
spoken.

Parable

Another month and a bit
more until the quietly
come and patient renewal
of adolescent branches
expanding in mid-
February gathers to
the same place again,
in pieces like the slow puffs
of sand that tag a desert
sunset; the ground still
creaking with scattered heats and
partly remembered
voices gossiping as, more
or less curious, they make
their way to him from
one town after another
(or so the gospel teller
records), snuffling idly at
the story he told
of the seed-carrier and
the various grounds, the luck
of the draw.

      And a little —
more than a little afraid
to believe; because that's where
the fear really is, inside;
that's the devil I don't quite
know —
      but think I do;
so he's the one I can blame,
my companion who carefully
warns me that any excess may
(probably will) lead to pain;
that too much God, in a word,
is as bad as too little;
that, finally, there isn't
much out there after all
our work is over,
beyond the palings.

It's still difficult
to distinguish their voices,
or questions, or gender
for that matter, either those
who piss against the wall
(as young David once put it)
or dribble in the dirt;
pieces and bits, with an hour
or two more to go and
"Ecoutez! Move it!" rumbling
through the slow again dark
where the houses almost leave
off and the road begins.

Lammas for T. R.

It's still early, the bulging walls
knobby with purples of morning
glory and even God's petals
are too soft to touch. Here he comes
around a corner of the house,
skirmishing between the puddles,
an old tune dying on a stone.

I'm itchy as green raspberries;
daft as a cat; a litle bit
tight in the pants, I guess; two sheets
into the wind — and I very
much believe that a red-headed
woman is the cause of it all.

Do you hear me? you, Theodore
Roethke, raunching, goose-footed hulk
booming through the rain; do you hear?
you, squawking like a gull, mangy-
sweet-miracle, muddy as spring;
you floppy rose, does the heron
know where you are?
                    (or how this voice
as treacherous as ecstasy
relieves for another minute
or two the something, the other
that glares like crinkles of limestone
into the lean, unwilling dark)

These shadows are geting twitchy
again; it must be nearly noon;
and two birds skimming my window
in long familiar strokes after
the rain, to pull it together
and not quite themselves yet, trying
a new kind of balance and like
a girl's breasts running too fast, stops,
blushing in a whoop of sunlight,
becoming frightened of themselves.

I walked as far as November
one day; it was, as I recall,
a lonely place. My despair is
separate from candles. I wake
upward. The lake is my distance.
Too soft a grass stain cripples me.

After all, neither night nor day
would have any sense to make if
somebody like me didn't need
any sense to be made into,
droopy and tense at the same time
like a prayer of marigolds;
they are soft and broken looking
with a dusty thin glaze over
the different yellows and browns,
and there is nothing in the whole
world as silent as they are now,
not even the old wooden wind.

I am responsible as wax.
Whose footsteps do I touch? I
am as ignorant as a stream;
becoming also somewhat more
forgetful of late, I've begun
to count each morning along with
the eggs and milk, but still manage
to misplace them. Who is the bell?

I brush away the dust neatly
after each new Apocalypse.
I speak to skeletons only
when I'm spoken to first and wait
till evening to cross the desert,
taking one or two warm sweaters
and a carefully wrapped apple.

from **Theseus Remembered**

Carefully now
in each the lost hour
anticipating how
the artifice of spoken light
repeats the entered year
in each the year's ending;
the idiot and husk
of Theseus the Athenian
flaccid waiting at the grove
of hell.

He mutters softly into
the wrinkled dark. The shadows
that you see or seem to see
are ghosts within this stone
of once known things. In this place
of tenuous awareness,
the anarchy of sensation,
vital sightings are recalled,
stripped now of wish and wonder,
idle similarities of truth:
physis kryptesthai philei
(where only the possible
is confined)
          *

          One
word, sea word broke his changing dream.
He rose with his dark brother.

A day or two, and
they encountered her beyond
the loosened river; descended
quietly over the sheer rocks
speckled with the hound's white breath.
They waited until evening
and moved on, into
their wilderness obscurely led.

They rested; sleeping first,
then eating when they woke.
The grass from Helene's
thin nates fall'n. They baked
a cake, divided water, ate
and drank; but the girl impatient,
sucking honey from her teeth, hopped
slowly on one leg, kicking
the loose dirt and spitting
brightly into the shadows.

Naiad

Almost unsayable now,
the bended light-to-shadows
of her casual exposing and
not quite green, the thick stem
urges into the river,
displacing softer grass.

Sweat or dew drop?
a something where
the scatter of quartz
in how many sidewalks
greying to "summer's
a bummer but — who"

and the dumber muscles
of these beech trees
stammer your name,
your soft hair and
softer
    and
the grey flash of water
at road's edge before
another day ends.

Lake Shuswap

The casually spaced
pale alder trees
defining position
and suspended
growth here, a kind
of not-place, heavy
as the certain air
and the long light falls;

shimmer of the lake,
and the sound of it
in some otherwhere
dividing, absorbing
each day again,
speckles of the fallen
leaves, moist dapple
and soft repeating trail.

Pastorale

There was a floated day:

     How
we set out one morning,
climbing eagerly away
from the smaller,
younger growth, clear trails,
over the mists contracting
and firm line of the lakeshore;

was light yet a little
obscured in the loose bush
heavier graced, and wended
cautiously a wren's bone
further to th' dimness of
what occasion was before
the parted way, half
found, half made;
     until
we broke into a soft,
the hidden meadow, as
the casual coming light
of thickly curled 'em yellows
and blaze of shelter here
absconded, waits.

     (Is
ever a word of this doing
to strangely silence
in a place it cannot fill;
a piece of the long wind only;
this unconjurable grass.)

Hansel and Gretel
for Ken Stange

Everything different, everything the same.
They've both 'em come nearly so far as this
before, and manage to sign each turn with
a piece of "Nothing ventured, nothing found."

They wonder the morning it why again
till, brittle as bread, they're re-collected
and forgotten into a sorting way
together.

After a while, though, it's not
as easy to cross that field any more
or less predictably; or wonder who
which sign was meant, the raven or the dove
reselving; till finally, unable
to see anything, they begin to see.

Poetry too is biodegradable.

What the Bird Said

In primavera:

green is the apple tree
though notgreen I, having
no alterable substance
and rickety of mind
so patiently inclined
to falter into spring;

with no thing-
memory to load
the brittle catapult of truth,
only a quivering
sustains, a wonder choose.

Like a whistle of stars it was
when Myrlin stood mute
silver and silver in the grass.

In primavera is
a kind and gaining of
once upon the whole
it, choice and choosing,
delicate in this season

comes an only to be
and he contented yes
to watch the strangely shadow pass.

A winter dew drop wets my root,
rippling into some second truth.

Elegy
from the Old English

      There
is a dark house
greyleaf grows there
rime whitens edges
rueful the walls
torn and toppled
wasted by time
the scent of   rowan
is parted and past
leaving the dingle
quiet now;
a name written
on a dry stick
departing

Black Spruce with Raven

for Mary Weymark Goss

There are holes at the edge
of this forest, partings,
interruptions of what
marks of a feather only did
the silence in's making leave.

Not only these shapes, but
a something scattered (may be)
through the working dust, echoes
of that own death, the pattern
seenless, stumbled into,
tentatively claimed.

      And
are now this such and sorting
in th' old familiar pulse
of (must be) to each a mute
deception gained?

      yet
are known they, the wonder,
and all the words whose crinkle
a minute determines
the enter (both, be) and breach
to placid my westering.

   *

How each taken thing
a kind in's place regains
the time and singly token
of our stammer'd going;
and how again the touch
surprizes, or even's the end
of whatever wobble I reach to?

46

So. The dark thing
crumbles, is recognized;
and the long bird urging
part and parts to, over
this tangle of known trees.

Owl Light

Wind-caught, and persistently a faint smell
of decay, the plunge abruptly between
the careful folding of this darkness with
a kind of entering remembered,
                    drops
through noiselessly her breaking alphabet
to claim my trickle and last movings; as
the pubic curl of beak, a glitterand
reflection on the separating dirt.

"It's strange," you said, "the things that come to mind
when you smell death." The middle place between
the alien and known: Is this the where
our last identity endures? common
as grace, perhaps, and unexpectedly
its tendons loosen and grow warm.

                    But
there's no way to hold the folded skull who
will never dream it exactly, that dream
again. Only the possible remains.

And deepens now into another hour
before the final agitation: or
a smudge of ash against my thinning bone.
These my traces only as
carefully the mild
erumpent moon in here this code
and open prism of it selved, relumes.

Nocturne I

Into these own familiar
and mumbled shadows
shape 'em quietly
the ending day, till
certain a little and
partially the edges
opening.

Fingers of wood smoke.
The fume reminds me, fickle
with meaning as a turned stone.

We come to our selving
accidentally, it seems;
and how an hour or so
as the decorous jaw line
of the long sky equally
in unexpected stars
thickens another name to be.

Oddly the interchange;
though I'm a sort
of nearer to it now,
that broken summer
and separating task,
uncertain again but
careful here as deer moving
dusk-wise out from mist
to follow some further
my forms and symbols, where they lead.

Nocturne II
for H. A. Williams

The shaking here, distorted mass
of the late garden fills slowly
and a cluster of Japanese
Lanterns crisply appearing as
my eyes re-focus, accepting
the edges of the night.

       A touch
redeems, and pop's my weasel when
the sudden flash of a herb bag
scalded, calls without naming, as
the body its own truth darkly
authenticates image and claim.

All knowing's such a mystery
perhaps, a losing to find, if
wholly the unsuspecting dream
where is a vein for silver (or
even here a gaining chance) or
where the unended day renews.

Flowering Ivy

Containing . . .
     or the way I went through,
a not-place of seeing that stays now
neither inside nor outside, like
the boundaries of Matisse's
Flowering Ivy, irrelevant
to whether the edge moves forward or back.

Somewhere beyond that flower, say, not
quite recognizable yet;
or flower is made possible only
by whatever it is not;

       or neither
makes any more difference than the duff
of wet pine needles without
conspicuous colour, a place
that (say me) does not echo or recall.

Varieties of Religious Experience
for Amy Friedman

Reaching defines that grasp: the argument
from design; though there's not much difference
between one desert and another when
you're passing through; and something falling in
the pause between . . . bell strokes.

                   Or dump
'em there, a thousand or so beans, say, as
W J suggested, mix and pick
till you can get anything you want —
but found, hear, once, is lost again never;

till search is the centre for who or what
a casual description, maybe, and
the dark articulations of bamboo
seen briefly, pollen drifting, interweaves
. . . but when that bell stroke?

The Burning Bush

No one's life, according to Joseph K,
stretches long enough to enter Canaan;
piecings and Pisgah sights sufficient till
such that loss acknowledged, heals.

The evening
silent now of birds; the morning and what
after the dew gone. Word, then, if image
deceives, though what that coming word may be
I do not know.

    He remembers oddly
his first enflamement: sight of in splotches
Loranthus creepy crawling one death at
a time. "Take off your shoes!"

            My toes contain
holiness, distinguishing part and part,
and is enough a stone's throw further to
the edges of improbable daylight.

Like Trees, Walking
in mem. W.J. Barnes

It was the only time he had to try
it twice (as if the story breath by breath
exposing). They move delicately to
the edge of town, making a miracle
from bits and spits whose speakable mixture
as before in eden garden moistured
when "What do you see?" to first for naming
in a shuffle of trees.

       A funny thing
divided me this evening on my way
to the Apocalypse. Here too the wonder,
did it happen or did anything else
ever happen? confronts to a gaining
till something human this way comes and here
they are, those grinning trees, like men, standing.

Ghazal for Kim

It doesn't matter what size the house
as long as you can walk around it.

The trail widens, narrows again;
one step at a time.

Quiet enough now, after
the branch stops trembling.

The heron gliding overhead
in a slow explosion of air.

Out of sight — but even the poke
of this blackberry sags a bit.

Curls of them, the small grass
patient in yet this sunlight.

Your bare legs unmoving:
do I lead or follow?

Goings
in mem. Bronwen Wallace

For a minute or so Judas forgets
why he'd come into the story,
with one end of the garden
much like the other

and at the bottom of the hill,
that final twist of South,
the corner at Marine,
stuns a hair's breath nearer clarity
and neither in this place or other
and pick it up ruefully,
accusing (falsely) a splayed pebble
   "No, not I."

The poet brushes aside
an imaginary screen of gnats:
she knows there are other ways
of translating the passage, but
here's near enough;
and she sits another hour or so
watching exactly
how a garlic flower looks.

The Rocks

Later that afternoon,
the pool of Koi fish
collecting, distributing shadows,
till a water spider briskly
and the merge of cedar branches
thicker and smelling
of something other -- strawberries?

       We used
to call it The Rocks,
but never went back
after that day -- the almost seen who but
running again and running to clasps of
the short, grey moss, slipping, too clumsy
and still cannot and he was screaming and
  "It was a signal,"
  he explained.

     And this evening
the pale young girl will sit
quietly in her
very own corner
of the restaurant.

The Field

Each scurry's a little different now . . .

and the ground still dry with it,
that dinned, proleptic echo
charioting,

         but which occasion this?
(He was much quieter after I killed
him) if the wary encumbering of
bent vines, hungry in the clotted heat and
pacing a discovery of here
the day's new and racketing limit,

         and
that sense again, as T R suggested,
that each image hints totally
its here and alien expansions
for the quickening
and dying, doubly known.

The Consul

Not yet.

        But once
as I was walking by
some pale strawbits
at the start of the field
and each word more slowly
in a language I didn't understand
or notice if the field had ended.

        I and my other?
perhaps, or both within /
without, a spiritual giddiness
or kind of prevenient fluttering
about the edges,
living in all worlds, occupying none,
till I am become in which new choice
of my own returning.

        But thou, Lord,
how long before the wound
that never quite closes and
the Consul regarding how
two or more shadows through the garden.

Badlands

for Robert Hilles

We walked together into the badlands
some forty days or so, but then — I don't
know how — I lost track of him. Everything
different, everything the same, and me still
searching my nothings, I guess, just bummin'
along for the ride.

                 That wind again. What
was it he used to say? "You can't see much
out here, but keep your ears open — your fears
as well, and don't grope it, the outering,
inescapable, but where the only
catch may and thrive 'em between yr wet bones
blindly."

                 The air balanced, shifts. He opens
his hands carefully, spreading the fingers
until there are dark places between them.

Near Ruby Lake
for John Pass & Theresa Kishkan

So if each day dies with (as
the Jesuit tells), then what cost the news
I skirmished an early this morning —

and again the tree frog
resonant with everything not yet
understood:

"And get off by the lake,"
you said, "step carefully,
but not *too* carefully, and let
the stone weigh a little before
skipping" —

           or yet to be?
if this last my loosening, or
another hour suspended here,
extends through the small hairs
of this pale grass and the rock

is parted and the cling of
this extravagant, tremulous word
darkens and turns to each
unknowing, newly, so.

Manresa

I expect it looked pretty much
like a Travelodge — nothing new, really,
mostly a cutting back — keep
the image small.

        Remember,
never trust a man
whose voice changes when
he talks about God

        (like
when a guy puts his hand on your shoulder
only he's thinking lower)

        and
the monk's prayer (says Anthony)
is not perfected until
he can't remember it.

How Shall I Explain?
after Han Shan

Hold
the stone and I am in it; split
the branch and you divide me.

Remember that cold mountain guy?
he used to say things like that,
or "Gargle before you spit."
A bit
of what the ever's passing through
town this evening, I hear,
between the Fingers
and a quarter south of Desolation.

Watch out for flotsam but remember,
just because it's broken doesn't mean
you've got to fix it.

After a frizzle or two
the candle regains its equanimity.

*

He takes a quick inventory of the relevant bones
and bits (Now I lay me downly), listens for a mo
to the sounds of one gull flying around the harbour
before the madness is complete.

He has nothing
in particular to say this morning,
pole and pebble equally
mute as a fruit (Let me finish),
frail as the Southern Cross, that oddly
embarrased structure in the undulating night.

He goes for a walk because his pants are wet.
Even the crows have forgotten where he lives.

As Once

Still somewhat deceptive
as:

           the boat turning
between those three branches
a little each time and
the water grey and grey,
dimensionless

        unless
that airy skeleton
mucking slowly about
in the middle of things

         (what
Johann called being at
the centre of the harmonies)

without paying any
particular attention to where
or there's the place
my final decorous birds
ascending

        once upon
a walking along the path
in these new woods, blackberries.